KT-226-257

Author:
Fiona Macdonald studied History at
Cambridge University and at the University
of East Anglia. She has taught in schools,
adult education and university, and is the
author of numerous books for children on
historical topics.

Series creator:
David Salariya was born in Dundee,
Scotland. He has illustrated a wide range of
books and has created and designed many
new series for publishers both in the U.K.
and overseas. In 1989 he established The
Salariya Book Company. He lives in Brighton
with his wife, the illustrator Shirley Willis,
and their son Jonathan.

Editors:
Karen Barker Smith
Stephanie Cole

© The Salariya Book Company Ltd MMII
All rights reserved. No part of this book may be reproduced
stored in a retrieval system or transmitted in any form or
by any means, electronic, mechanical, photocopying,
recording or otherwise, without the written permission
of the copyright owner.

Created, designed and produced by
The Salariya Book Company Ltd
25 Marlborough Place,
Brighton BN1 1UB
Please visit us at:
www.salariya.com
www.book-house.co.uk

Published in Great Britain in 2002 by Hodder Wayland,
an imprint of Hodder Children's Books

A catalogue record for this book is available from
the British Library.

ISBN 0 7502 3588 8

Printed and bound in Spain.

Printed on paper from sustainable forests.

Hodder Children's Books
A division of Hodder Headline Limited
338 Euston Road, London NW1 3BH

Picture credits
t=top b=bottom c=centre r=right l=left

Archaeological Receipts Fund, Athens: 18tl,
29c, 39b
British Museum: 8bl, 11bl, 13t, 13b, 15c, 16bl,
17tr, 20tl, 20br, 22bl, 24bc, 25r, 27tr, 31tr, 32bl,
35tr, 37r, 41c, 42b
John Foxx Images:7b

Additional artists
Giovanni Caselli   John James
Nick Hewetson   David Stewart
Pam Hewetson   Gerald Wood

GODS & GODDESSES

IN THE DAILY LIFE OF THE

ANCIENT GREEKS

Written by Fiona Macdonald

Illustrated by Dave Antram
and Mark Bergin

HODDER
Wayland

an imprint of Hodder Children's Books

CONTENTS

INTRODUCTION

Worship was very important in ancient Greece; it was part of everyday life. Men, women and children said prayers, made offerings and took part in religious festivals. They visited temples, where gods and goddesses lived. They also asked for divine help at times such as births, weddings and funerals.

The Greeks worshipped many different kinds of gods and goddesses. Some were nature-spirits, living in mountains, forests and streams. Others were local or tribal gods, who watched over just one city or clan. A few were 'borrowed' from neighbouring peoples. But the best-known and most powerful group of gods and goddesses was the 'family' headed by Zeus and his wife Hera. Known as the 'Olympians', because they lived on Mount Olympus in northern Greece, legends told how they fought and conquered earlier, more primitive, gods – the Titans, children of Uranus (heaven) and Gaia (earth).

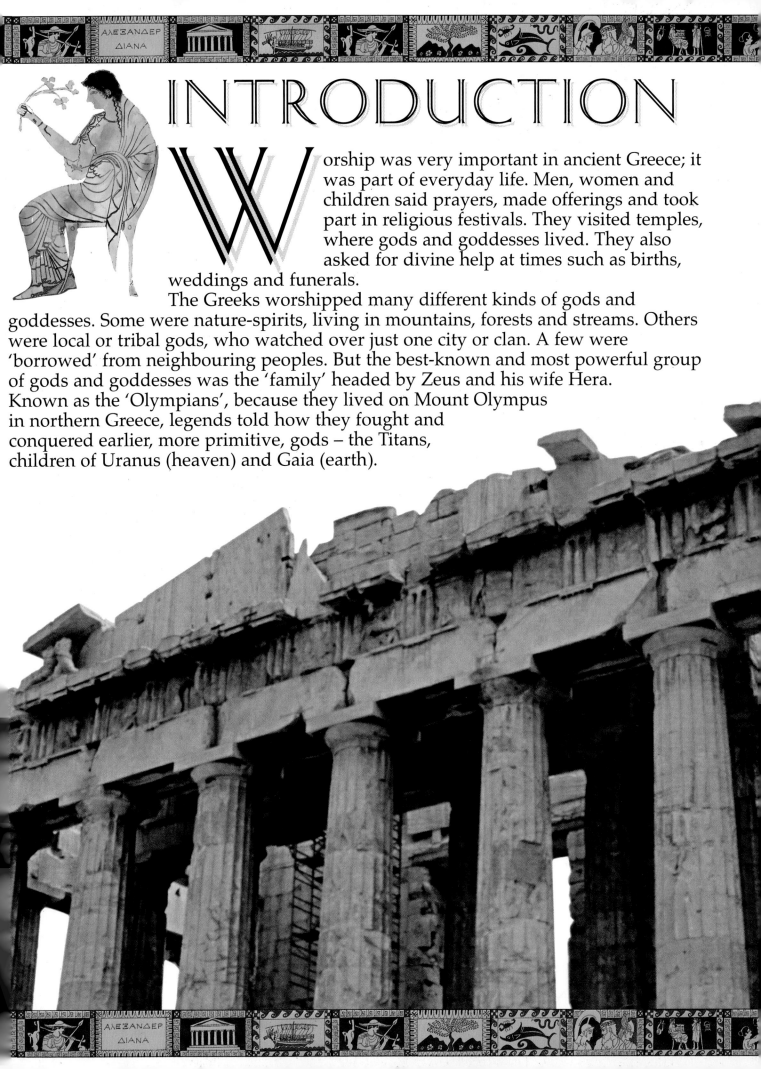

ZEUS
KING OF THE GODS: LAWS AND GOVERNMENT

On this painted vase (below) made in Athens in the 5th century BC, Zeus is shown seated on his royal throne. His son Hephaestus stands behind him, and his daughter Athena is shown emerging from his head.

Zeus was king of the gods. Ancient Greek myths tell how he brought order to the world by defeating his father, Cronus, and the whole race of Titans. From Mount Olympus, Zeus ruled over heaven and earth. He was honoured as the defender of Greek civilisation. He upheld justice and the law, and punished wrongdoers by hurling thunderbolts at them. He was the guardian of friendship and hospitality. He also controlled the weather.

In this statue (above), Zeus holds a thunderbolt in his right hand and a long sceptre in his left. The goddess Nike crowns him with laurel leaves.

FAMILY

Father Cronus
Mother Rhea
Wives Metis and Hera
Children Athena, Ares, Eileithyia, Hebe, Hephaestus (and many others)
Brothers Hades, Poseidon
Sisters Demeter, Hera, Hestia

Athena

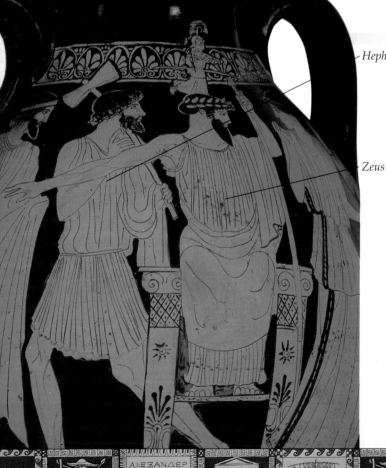

Hephaestus

Zeus

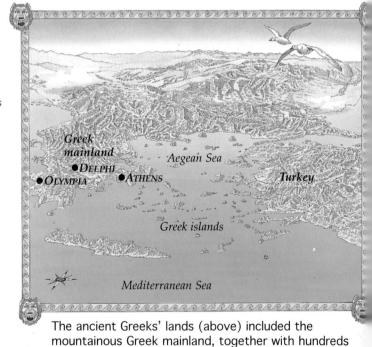

The ancient Greeks' lands (above) included the mountainous Greek mainland, together with hundreds of nearby islands and colonies in Sicily, southern France, north Africa and the western coast of Turkey.

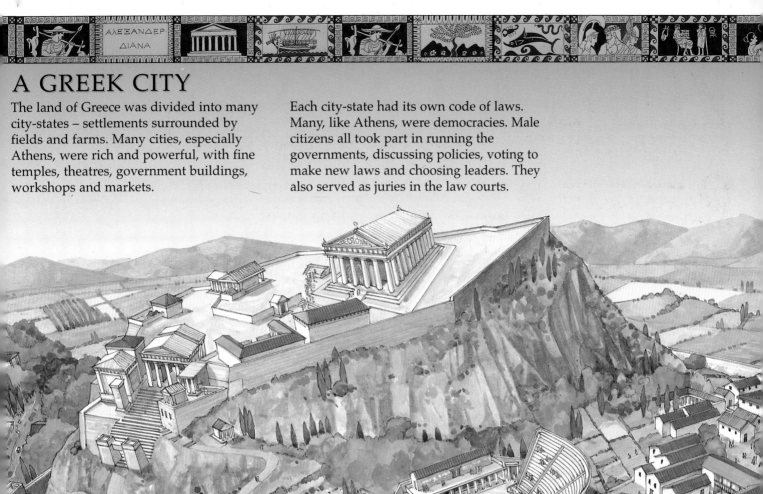

A GREEK CITY

The land of Greece was divided into many city-states – settlements surrounded by fields and farms. Many cities, especially Athens, were rich and powerful, with fine temples, theatres, government buildings, workshops and markets.

Each city-state had its own code of laws. Many, like Athens, were democracies. Male citizens all took part in running the governments, discussing policies, voting to make new laws and choosing leaders. They also served as juries in the law courts.

HESTIA
GODDESS OF THE HEARTH: HOUSE AND HOME

Hestia watched over homes and hearth. When a baby was born, it was carried round the hearth, to symbolize its acceptance into the family that gathered beside the hearth-fire. Greek cities kept a fire burning to honour Hestia in important government buildings. Officials made sacrifices there on behalf of all the citizens, and fire from the holy flame was given to warriors setting out on campaigns.

Hestia

Hestia was also worshipped in splendid temples at the holy shrines of Delphi (right) and Olympia, where thousands of pilgrims journeyed to ask special favours from the gods. Settlers leaving Greece to found colonies overseas took fire from Hestia's temples with them, so that she would watch over their new homes there.

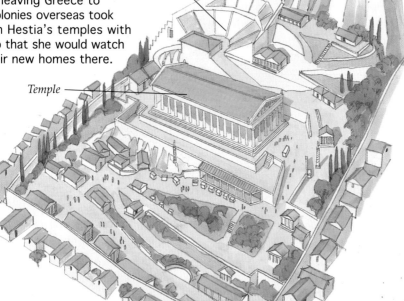

Theatre

Temple

INSIDE STORY
Hestia was a pure, solitary goddess. Both Poseidon and Apollo wanted to marry her. She refused them, and asked Zeus to protect her, vowing to remain a virgin forever. Zeus agreed and gave her special blessings in return. He ordered that she was to be worshipped in every household, and honoured at all feasts.

A GREEK HOME

Greek homes reflected traditional beliefs and values. Each house had an altar, where prayers were said, and a hearth where a fire was kept constantly burning. Greeks from wealthy or noble families believed that it was wrong for women to appear in public, so there were separate women's rooms, as well as a dining room where men could entertain male friends.

Greek houses (below) were made of rough stone or mud brick, which might be covered with a thick layer of plaster and supported by stone foundations for extra protection. Roofs were made of slate, or, more often, baked clay tiles. Floors and windows were made from planks of rough wood; wood was also used for window shutters. Window-glass was unknown. Many houses had courtyards, to provide fresh air and space for a cooking fire. Large homes had upper storeys, reached by a simple wooden ladder, instead of stairs.

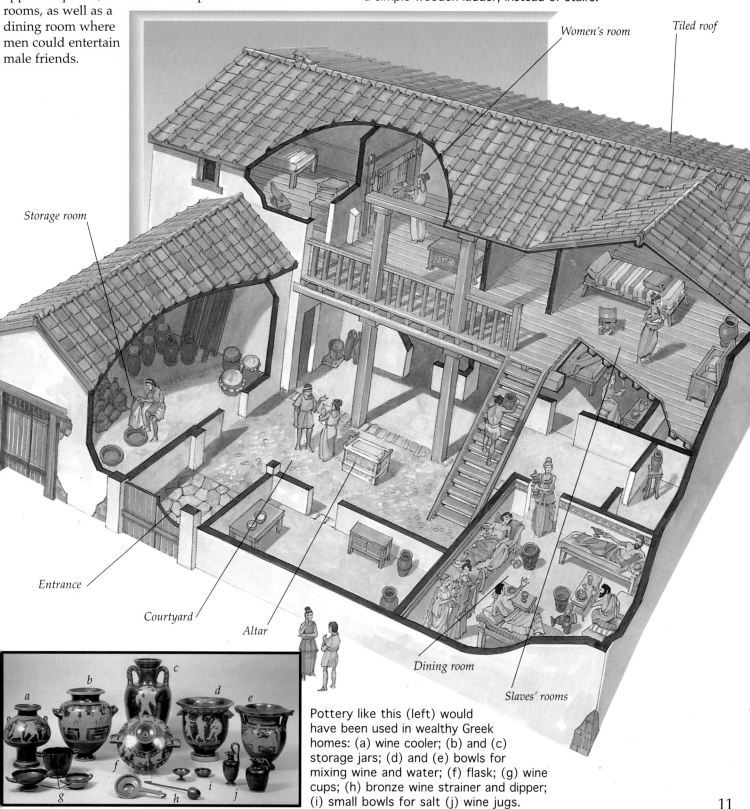

Women's room

Tiled roof

Storage room

Entrance

Courtyard

Altar

Dining room

Slaves' rooms

Pottery like this (left) would have been used in wealthy Greek homes: (a) wine cooler; (b) and (c) storage jars; (d) and (e) bowls for mixing wine and water; (f) flask; (g) wine cups; (h) bronze wine strainer and dipper; (i) small bowls for salt (j) wine jugs.

HERA
WIFE OF ZEUS: GREEK WOMEN'S LIVES

Hera was the wife and sister of Zeus. Queenly and beautiful, she was the goddess of marriage and motherhood. Women asked her to protect them and bring them happiness in their married lives. Hera's own marriage was very unhappy. Her husband, Zeus, chased other women and often left her alone, feeling miserable. Hera showed her anger by nagging her husband and by arranging terrible punishments for the women he loved.

FAST TRACK	
Ares	p 26
Demeter	p 20
Hades	p 36
Hephaestus	p 16
Hestia	p 10
Poseidon	p 28
Zeus	p 8

Greek women used mirrors made of polished metal. They stored perfumed ointments, face-powder and rouge in pottery boxes and jars (above). These were often decorated with pictures of women's lives.

Greek women wore long, loose robes made from wool, linen or silk. They were bound around the waist by a girdle of cloth. Married women tied up their hair in knots and coils, or covered it with veils.

FAMILY
Father Cronus
Mother Rhea
Husband Zeus
Children Ares,
  Eielithyia, Hebe,
  Hephaestus
Brothers Zeus,
  Hades, Poseidon
Sisters Demeter,
  Hestia

Hydra

Heracles

INSIDE STORY
Hera could be very cruel. She persecuted the hero Heracles, son of Zeus and a human princess, Alcmene, all his life. First she sent snakes to kill Heracles while he was still a baby, but, miraculously, he strangled them. Later, when Heracles was a man, Hera made the hundred-headed Hydra (left) attack him.

If they could afford it, Greek women liked to wear necklaces, earrings and bracelets of silver and gold. They also pinned golden flowers in their hair. Some jewellery, like this gilded pottery necklace (below) was made especially to decorate dead bodies when they were buried. It has survived until today, and provides valuable evidence to tell us what other pieces of Greek jewellery, worn by living women, might have looked like.

Gilded pottery necklace

MARRIAGE

Marriage was the only career open to Greek women. Girls were married when they were about 13 or 14 years old, often to men who were much older. Marriages were usually arranged by families; girls were not free to choose. When she married, a girl passed from the authority of her father to her husband's control. She had few legal rights of her own. The Greeks believed that the main purpose of marriage was to provide a son and heir to carry on the family name. A husband could divorce a wife who failed in this important female duty.

The wedding procession

On their wedding day, Greek brides were bathed and dressed in clean new clothes. Their hair was beautifully arranged, and, if their family could afford it, they were decked in jewels. Then they were led from their parents' house to the home of their husband's family in a torchlight procession at dusk, as shown on this pot (right). Sometimes they rode in a chariot pulled by horses, while attendants shouted joyful cries of 'Io hymen!'

ATHENA
GODDESS OF WISDOM: CRAFTS AND SKILLS

Athena was the goddess of wisdom, cleverness and crafts. According to legend, she sprang fully-grown from the head of Zeus, after he swallowed her pregnant mother, Metis. Athena was one of the most active of Greek goddesses. She guided women's crafts, especially spinning and weaving, and work done by Greek men, such as carpentry, shipbuilding and pottery-making. She invented the *aulos* (double flute) and taught humans how to grow olive trees.

Athena was a goddess of war and protector of Athens. In the 5th century BC, Athens paid for a temple called the Parthenon to be built in her honour. It housed this magnificent statue (above).

FAMILY
Father Zeus
Mother Metis
Uncles Poseidon, Hades
Aunts Hestia, Hera, Demeter
Grandfather Cronus
Grandmother Rhea

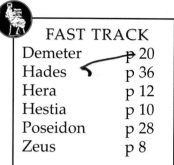

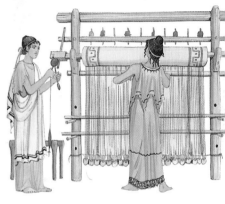

Women spun thread and wove it into cloth for their families to wear (above). They also made blankets and rugs for their homes

Greek potters (below) were famous throughout Mediterranean lands. Their pots, made of red clay with black and white glazes, were decorated with pictures of everyday life or with scenes of myths and legends featuring gods, heroes and monsters. Most pots were made in small workshops, close to potters' homes. The whole family, and their slaves, joined in the work.

INSIDE STORY
Athena had a special favourite called Jason. He was a hero who sailed north in search of a magical Golden Fleece. Ancient myths tell how Athena helped woodworker Argus to build a boat (right) for Jason's voyage. It contained a plank of oak from the holy sanctuary at Dodona. The plank could speak, and give wise advice.

CRAFTWORKERS

Towns and cities in Greece were home to skilled craftworkers of many different kinds. Some produced solid, hard wearing goods for ordinary families to use; others created rare, splendid masterpieces for rich patrons to admire.

Without big machines to help workers, all craft goods were made by hand, using human muscle power. The most famous and respected craftworkers and artists led semi-nomadic lives, moving from place to place to work on major carvings and sculptures, or to supervise the construction of splendid new buildings.

Potters used thin 'slip' clay to decorate pots with pictures in red, black and white.

Sculptors used hammers and sharp chisels to carve life-like statues from stone.

Basket-makers wove strong containers from thin twigs and plaited straw.

Leatherworkers used knives, needles and thread to make shoes, bags and hats.

Building the boat for Jason's voyage in search of the Golden Fleece

HEPHAESTUS

GOD OF FIRE: METALWORKING

FAMILY

Father Zeus
Mother Hera
Wife Aphrodite
Children Erichthonius,
  Periphetes, Cabiri,
  Palaemonius
Brother Ares
Sisters Eileithyia,
  Hebe

Hephaestus used his mighty blacksmith's axe to assist the gods in many ways. For example, he helped Zeus give birth to the goddess Athena by splitting open his skull (below), so that Athena could escape. Hephaestus used more delicate skills to build palaces for the gods and to create golden robots, that worked for him in his forge on Mount Olympus.

Hephaestus was the god of fire and metalworking. He turned rock into deadly bronze weapons or into beautiful gold jewellery. After being thrown off Mount Olympus by Hera, his mother, he lived for nine years in a cave by the sea, practising his metalworking skills. Then, to punish Hera, he made her a golden throne which trapped her as soon as she sat in it. Hephaestus was worshipped in busy cities like Athens. Legends said that he lived in volcanoes.

INSIDE STORY

For many years, only the gods had fire. A famous myth tells how Prometheus, a Titan, first brought fire to Earth by stealing it from Mount Olympus and hiding it in a hollow fennel-stalk. When Zeus found out, he was very angry and sentenced Prometheus to a horrible punishment. He was chained to a rock, where, every day, an eagle came to tear out his liver. After many years, the hero Heracles found a way of ending Prometheus's torture. He shot the eagle, and set Prometheus free.

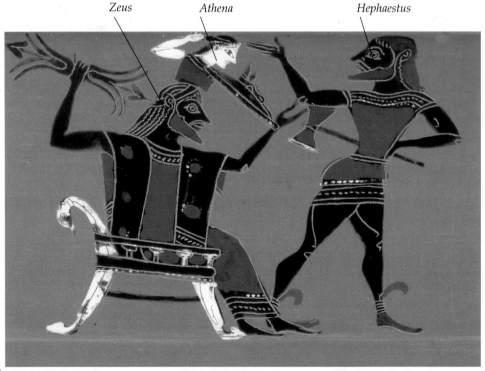

Zeus   Athena   Hephaestus

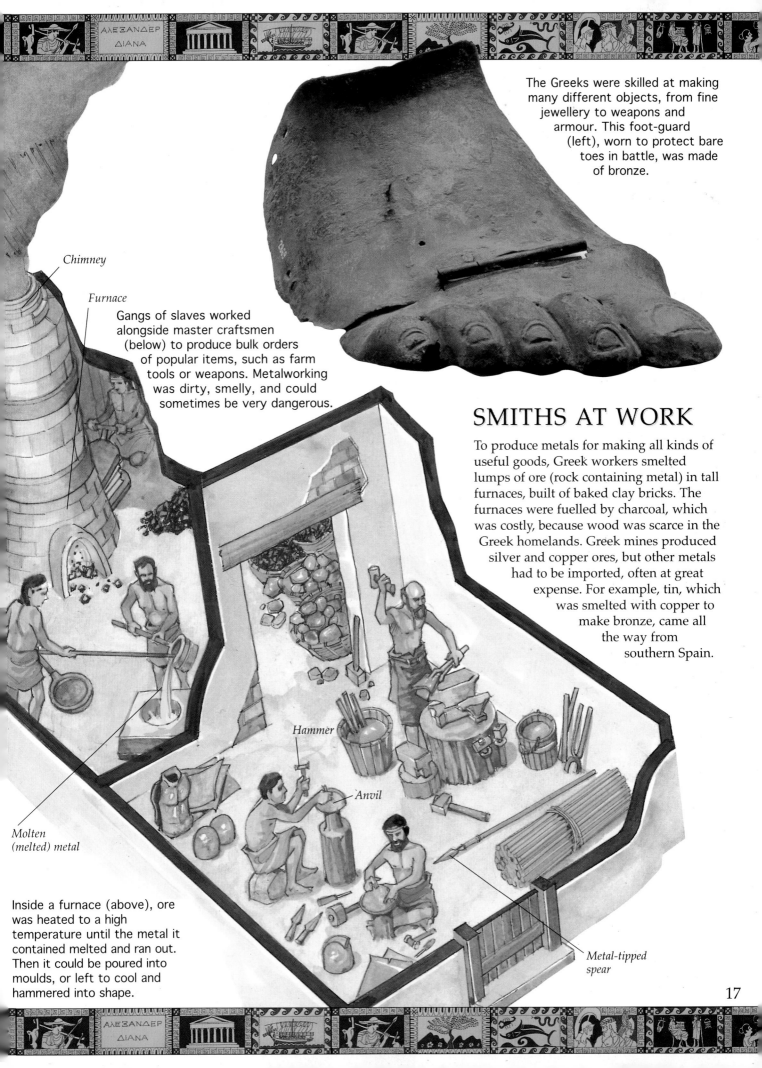

The Greeks were skilled at making many different objects, from fine jewellery to weapons and armour. This foot-guard (left), worn to protect bare toes in battle, was made of bronze.

Chimney

Furnace

Gangs of slaves worked alongside master craftsmen (below) to produce bulk orders of popular items, such as farm tools or weapons. Metalworking was dirty, smelly, and could sometimes be very dangerous.

SMITHS AT WORK

To produce metals for making all kinds of useful goods, Greek workers smelted lumps of ore (rock containing metal) in tall furnaces, built of baked clay bricks. The furnaces were fuelled by charcoal, which was costly, because wood was scarce in the Greek homelands. Greek mines produced silver and copper ores, but other metals had to be imported, often at great expense. For example, tin, which was smelted with copper to make bronze, came all the way from southern Spain.

Hammer

Anvil

Molten (melted) metal

Inside a furnace (above), ore was heated to a high temperature until the metal it contained melted and ran out. Then it could be poured into moulds, or left to cool and hammered into shape.

Metal-tipped spear

HERMES
THE MESSENGER: TRAVEL AND TRADE

As the messenger of the gods, Hermes often travelled between Heaven and Earth. However, he also had another, very special, duty – leading dead souls (above) from Earth to the Underworld, their final home. He was given a special title when performing this task – Hermes Psychopompus.

Many Greek cities had an open-air market place (right). Farmers, fishermen, merchants and craftworkers all brought their produce here to sell. From the 6th century BC, they used coins for trading.

Hermes was bright, talented and quick-witted – he invented the lyre – and he could be very charming, too. Zeus chose him to be his messenger and spy, keeping a lookout and carrying news between the gods on Mount Olympus and the humans far below. Because he made so many journeys, Hermes came to be worshipped as the god of travellers, and also of merchants, who travelled long distances, buying and selling their goods.

INSIDE STORY
Hermes was one of the few gods or men who had been to the Underworld and back. The Underworld was a chilly, gloomy place ruled by the god Hades. A few souls, who had lived good lives, enjoyed everlasting bliss in a part of the Underworld called the Elysian Fields. Those who had lived bad lives went to a region called Tartarus, which was a place of punishment and eternal suffering.

Shoppers (mostly men and servants) also came to the market place to talk and meet their friends. They liked to share news and discuss politics.

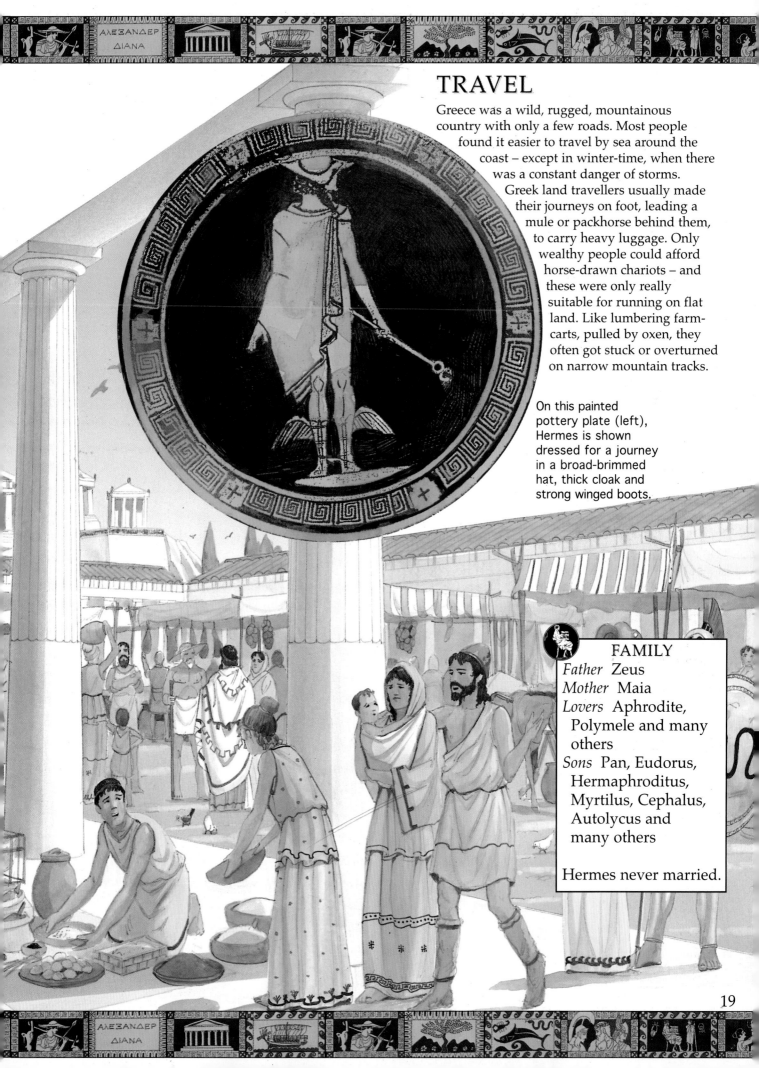

TRAVEL

Greece was a wild, rugged, mountainous country with only a few roads. Most people found it easier to travel by sea around the coast – except in winter-time, when there was a constant danger of storms.

Greek land travellers usually made their journeys on foot, leading a mule or packhorse behind them, to carry heavy luggage. Only wealthy people could afford horse-drawn chariots – and these were only really suitable for running on flat land. Like lumbering farm-carts, pulled by oxen, they often got stuck or overturned on narrow mountain tracks.

On this painted pottery plate (left), Hermes is shown dressed for a journey in a broad-brimmed hat, thick cloak and strong winged boots.

FAMILY
Father Zeus
Mother Maia
Lovers Aphrodite, Polymele and many others
Sons Pan, Eudorus, Hermaphroditus, Myrtilus, Cephalus, Autolycus and many others

Hermes never married.

DEMETER
GODDESS OF CORN: FOOD AND FARMING

Greek farms produced crops of grain, olives and wool. Most were used by farmers' families, but slaves (above) carried any surplus to market to sell.

INSIDE STORY
Demeter had a daughter called Persephone. One day, Persephone was snatched by the god Hades and taken to the Underworld – Hades wanted to marry her. Demeter was very sad and the world mourned with her. It went cold and dark and no plants grew. At last, Zeus sent Hermes to bring Persephone back. Demeter was overjoyed – but because Persephone had eaten in the Underworld, she could not stay on Earth. She had to live with Hades for a few months each year. When that happened, it was winter.

Demeter was the goddess of all growing things. The Greeks believed that she gave the gift of grain to humans, and also the first-ever fig tree. Unlike many other Greek gods, whose temples stood on high, wide-open places, Demeter was worshipped in ceremonies hidden underground. These were centred at the village of Eleusis, in southern Greece. Demeter was also honoured at a special women-only festival, the *Thesmophoria*, held in Athens once a year.

The vase below shows Demeter (standing left) and her beloved daughter Persephone (standing right) on either side of Triptolemus (seated, centre). He was a young man from Eleusis, near Athens, whom Demeter chose to carry her gifts of grain and agriculture to the world. He travelled in a chariot pulled by winged dragons; you can see one, perched on the chariot wheel.

Demeter

Winged dragon

Persephone

Triptolemus

FARMING

Most Greeks lived on country farms or in villages by the sea. They made a living as farmers and fishermen. Olives (right) were one of the most important crops. They were crushed to make oil, used in cooking, for burning in lamps, and for beauty care.

FAMILY
Father Cronus
Mother Rhea
Brothers Hades, Poseidon, Zeus
Sisters Hera, Hestia
Lovers Zeus, Iasion, Poseidon
Daughters Persephone, Despoina
Sons Plutus, Philomelus, Areion

Farmhouses (above) were small and simple, with rough walls of brick or stone, and tiled roofs.

Artemis was goddess of the countryside, wild animals, hunting and the moon. Like her twin brother Apollo, she was a skilful archer, shooting arrows that brought death to people throughout Greece. She had the power to heal, and fiercely defended people who worshipped her. Artemis spent her days hunting, playing with wild creatures, practising sports and bathing in hidden streams. Her companions were all virgins, like herself. She never married.

With well-trained dogs panting and straining at the leash, this huntsman (above) is returning home, carrying his prey. Favourite animals to hunt included wild boar, hare and deer.

INSIDE STORY

Artemis was quick to punish anyone who offended her. When Oeneus, King of Calydon, forgot to make the proper sacrifices at her temple, she sent a huge wild boar to terrorise his kingdom. It destroyed all the crops and killed people and farm animals. Oeneus's son called together all the best hunters in Greece to try and kill the Calydonian Boar. Many men and hunting dogs died in the chase, but at last the boar was cornered and killed. Its tusks were taken to Athena's temple, and its hide was put on display.

Wet nurse

Mother

Mothers in childbirth prayed to Artemis for help and protection. Brides also made offerings to her on the eve of their wedding. This was because, as a virgin, Artemis had never known the pain of giving birth. Looking after babies and children was one of Greek women's most important tasks. Wealthy women hired wet-nurses, as shown on this pot (left) and slaves to help feed their babies, and to make sure they were kept clean, warm and comfortable.

WILD CAUGHT FOOD

Most Greek food was produced on farms. However, wild foods from the countryside provided valuable extra nourishment, especially for poor people. They also supplied extra flavour and made plain dishes of bread or porridge more interesting. Poor people used snares, nets and sling-shots to catch little fish from streams, lizards and birds. They also gathered nuts, berries, wild mushrooms and herbs.

FAST TRACK	
Apollo	p 24
Athena	p 14
Zeus	p 8

FAMILY
Father Zeus
Mother Leto
Brother Apollo

Hunting with horses and hounds was a sport for rich people. Poor people usually went hunting on foot.

Hunters used dogs to track their prey through wild countryside, then shot at it with bows and arrows, or hurled their javelins towards it.

To kill their prey, hunters usually had to dismount. Stirrups had not yet been invented, which made it difficult to stay on the horse whilst stabbing at an animal.

Artemis was a deadly hunter. She even hunted humans who annoyed her. For example, when famous hunter Actaeon accidentally caught sight of Artemis naked while bathing, she turned him into a stag and told his own hounds to hunt him to death.

Artemis was a moon goddess. Like the moon itself, she was cold, remote and all-seeing. Hunters chose bright moonlit nights for chasing hare and deer. Poachers preferred to catch their prey on dark nights, when the moon was covered with clouds.

APOLLO
GOD OF MUSIC: THE ARTS AND EDUCATION

A teenage pupil (standing) and his teacher (seated) are portrayed on the base of a Greek cup (above). Only boys from rich families received a good education. Poor boys were taught their father's trade or craft skills. Girls learned spinning, weaving, housekeeping and babycare.

Greek boys started lessons when they were about 7 years old (above). They learned reading, writing, maths, music, dancing and sports. Older boys studied history, science, politics and philosophy, as well.

Greek artists always portrayed Apollo as a beautiful young man with short, curled hair and no beard. In this statue from the temple of Zeus at Olympia (right), he has a calm, stern and remote expression, to show that his thoughts are god-like and far above ordinary human concerns.

Apollo was the god of music and the arts as well as the god of prophecy. Often called Phoebus ('shining'), he was worshipped in some Greek cities as god of the Sun. Like his twin sister, Artemis, he protected animals, especially sheep and goats, and had the power to heal or to do harm. According to Greek myths, Apollo divided his time between Mount Olympus and Mount Parnassus, where the nine Muses spent their time enjoying music, poetry, dancing and many other arts.

FAMILY
Father Zeus
Mother Leto
Sister Artemis
Sons Asclepius, Orpheus, Aristeus, Philammon

INSIDE STORY
Apollo had many love affairs, with both goddesses and humans. One Greek story tells how Apollo desired Daphne, a beautiful young nymph. She did not love him and tried to run away. Apollo chased her and caught her. In despair, Daphne cried out to the other gods to save her. Zeus heard Daphne's cries and took pity on her. Just as Apollo seized Daphne in his arms, Zeus turned her into a laurel tree.

MUSIC

The Greeks believed that music had magic powers which could inspire love, soothe angry feelings, raise dull spirits or even tame wild animals and move heavy stones. They enjoyed singing, dancing and listening to music at feasts, family parties, theatre performances and religious festivals. Music echoed the feelings of people taking part in wedding and funeral processions and encouraged Greek soldiers as they marched off to war.

FAST TRACK	
Artemis	p 22
Asclepius	p 34
Zeus	p 8

Apollo often visited the Muses. They were nine beautiful goddesses who encouraged the arts. Terpsichore (shown on this painted Greek vase, right, playing a harp) was the Muse of dancing. The other Muses were Calliope (poetry), Clio (history), Euterpe (instrumental music), Thalia (comedy), Melpomene (tragedy), Erato (beautiful songs), Polymnia (serious songs, also mime), and Urania (astronomy).

The lyre (below left) was sacred to Apollo. It was made of a tortoise-shell, with strings of animal sinew or hide. Lyres were used to play solemn, serious music, or to accompany poets performing their work. Double pipes (below right) made a loud, cheerful sound. They were often played by slaves or dancing girls. One pipe produced the tune, the other made a background drone or hum.

Terpsichore

ARES

GOD OF WAR: BATTLES AND WEAPONS

FAMILY
Father Zeus
Mother Hera
Lovers Aphrodite,
  and many human
  women
Sons Deimos, Eros,
  Phobos and others
Daughter Penthesilia

Ares was the god of war, furious rage and mindless violence. He was strong, fierce and unable to control his temper or his actions when roused. Although he was handsome and very manly, he was not admired. Most Greeks valued a civilised, orderly way of living and hoped to spend their days working peacefully. They dreaded the chaos and suffering that war created. Few stories about Ares survive and none of them are pleasant. This tells us that Greek people preferred not to think about him if possible.

INSIDE STORY
Ares had an affair with Aphrodite, goddess of love. Aphrodite was married and when her husband, the god Hephaestus, found out that she loved Ares, he was furious. He made a metal net so fine that it could not be seen, and threw it over Ares and Aphrodite as they lay in bed together. The net trapped them. Hephaestus then called all the other gods to witness Ares's bad behaviour and Aphrodite's shame.

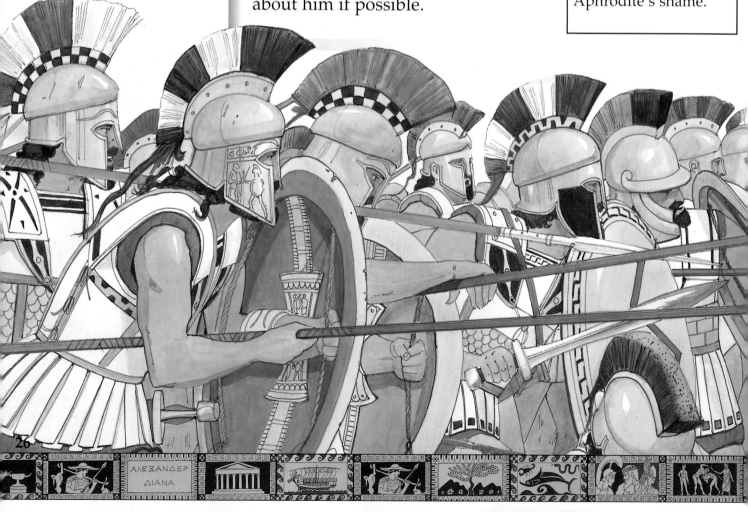

GREEKS AT WAR

Rival Greek city-states fought one another, as well as invading foreign enemies – especially the Persians, who lived in the land known today as Iran. All adult men were expected to fight to defend their homeland when it was attacked. Greek armies were made up mostly of foot-soldiers (called *hoplites*) who fought with swords and spears. They wore metal helmets, breastplates and greaves (shin-guards) as protection. Noblemen fought from chariots, or on horseback; poor men could only afford simple weapons such as sling-shots and stones. Sparta, in southern Greece, was especially famous for its tough soldiers. Its men – and women – were trained to fight from childhood.

In battle, *hoplite* soldiers fought in a phalanx – a close shoulder-to-shoulder line. Each man tried to protect himself and his comrades close by, while stabbing at the enemy with his sword or spear. So long as each man kept their place in the line, it was difficult for the enemy to break through, and advance.

This Greek vase (above), painted around 450 BC, shows soldiers from the city-state of Athens fighting against the Amazons, a tribe of women warriors who lived on the northern shores of the Black Sea. The Amazon warrior (shown on her knees) is carrying a battle-axe and a bow. Neither of these weapons was regularly used by the Greeks.

INSIDE STORY

Greek legends tell of a lost island called Atlantis that lay to the west of the Greek homelands. Once, Atlantis ruled a large empire in Europe and Africa, but it tried to make all its people into slaves. An alliance of free cities fought against it and destroyed it. Soon afterwards, Atlantis vanished below the waves and has never been seen again.

Poseidon was god of the sea, and, like the sea, he could be calm and gentle or rough and dangerous. The Greeks believed he could raise terrible storms – or calm them – by wielding his three-pronged trident. As well as ruling the sea, Poseidon was the god of earthquakes and tidal waves. Travellers on sea and land prayed to Poseidon and asked for his protection. Every two years, a sports festival, called the Isthmian Games, was held in his honour at the trading port of Corinth, in southern Greece.

FAMILY
Father Cronus
Mother Rhea
Wife Amphitrite
Brothers Zeus, Hades
Sisters Demeter, Hera, Hestia
Sons Orion, Theseus, Polyphemus (a cyclops), Pegasus (a winged horse) and many others.

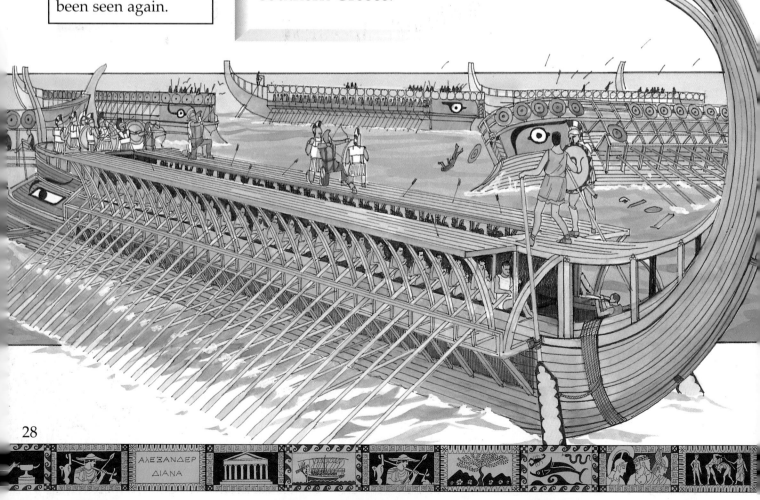

THE SEA IN DAILY LIFE

The sea played an important part in many Greek peoples' lives. Most towns and villages were built close to the coast or on islands. Fish and shellfish, caught fresh from the sea, provided the most important source of protein in most Greek families' meals. Travel by sea was also faster and easier than travel across the mountainous Greek mainland. The seas surrounding Greek lands were usually calm in summertime, but could be rough and stormy in winter. Shipwrecks and pirate raids were common. Even so, many Greeks earned their living as sailors or fishermen.

Greek ships (left) were powered by men rowing or by wind trapped in cloth sails.

The Greeks fought sea-battles by ramming enemy vessels with sharp metal 'beaks' fixed to the front of their own ships.

Confident and commanding, Poseidon gazes out across the waves. Greek artists liked to portray him as a handsome, middle-aged man, with rippling muscles and a splendid beard – to the Greeks, both were signs of masculine strength and power.

APHRODITE

GODDESS OF LOVE AND BEAUTY: CLOTHES AND JEWEL

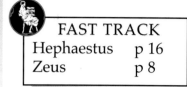

INSIDE STORY

Greek legend tells the extraordinary story of Aphrodite's birth. She was born from the waves after the god Cronus had attacked his father, Uranus, and flung his body parts into the sea. Foam gathered around them. Magically, this shaped itself into Aphrodite – the beautiful goddess of love. She floated ashore in Cyprus, or perhaps on the southern Greek island of Cythera.

Aphrodite was the goddess of love. She was beautiful, but thoughtless, unfaithful and dangerous too. She betrayed her husband and was not a good mother. She liked to meddle with the hearts and minds of everyone else and even her fellow gods and goddesses could not resist her charming powers. Aphrodite was also very vain and jealous of anyone else who looked beautiful. She invented horrid punishments for human women who boasted of their good looks.

FAST TRACK
Hephaestus   p 16
Zeus   p 8

FAMILY
Father Zeus
Mother Dione
Husband Hephaestus
Sons Deimos, Eros, Phobos and many others
Daughter Harmonia

Men doing hard physical work wore only a loincloth and a shady hat.

Outdoors, the Greeks wore sandals or boots.

Soldiers and travellers wore short cloaks.

Left: a *peplos* (short tunic). Right: a *chiton* (long tunic).

Women draped scarves and veils gracefully around their shoulders.

CLOTHING

Looking good was important in ancient Greece. The Greeks admired strong, healthy bodies, in men and women. Greek clothing styles were simple but elegant. Both sexes wore long, loose tunics, woven from linen and wool and coloured with dyes made from plants, insects and shellfish. In winter, they added woollen cloaks for extra warmth; in summer they wore shady hats of straw. Tunics and cloaks were held in place by pins, brooches and belts. Wealthy women also wore beautiful jewellery, especially bracelets, diadems (head-dresses) and earrings.

Golden hairpins, like this one (right), shaped like a spray of leaves and flowers, were very popular.

Rich women might wear gold earrings with pendants that jingled as the wearer moved (above).

They also wore bracelets, such as the one above, made of twisted gold wire decorated with animal heads.

In this scene from a painted cup (above), Aphrodite flies far above the troubled world of men and women on the back of a beautiful bird. Like the other Greek gods and goddesses, Aphrodite had favourites among humans, whom she tried to help. Sometimes, her interventions brought joy, but often they caused pain and even death. She sent Eros, her son, to shoot invisible arrows at her favourites, or victims. They made anyone they hit fall madly in love.

Women wore their hair long and arranged it in decorative coils and braids.

Sandals had thick soles made of cork and long leather laces.

Women covered themselves to avoid getting suntanned – a sign of slavery.

Rich people wore clothes decorated with embroidered borders.

Respectable women veiled their heads when they went outside their homes.

Farm workers wore warm boots and sheepskin caps in winter-time.

DIONYSUS
GOD OF WINE: DANCING AND THEATRE

Female followers of Dionysus (above) were known as *maenads* ('wild women'). They wore deerskins and wreaths of ivy – or live snakes! – and carried a *thyrsus* (magic wand) made of fennel stalks. They handled dangerous wild animals, like the leopard shown above. It was said that they ripped peaceful domestic animals limb from limb and devoured their flesh.

Dionysus was the god of wine and drunkenness. Greek legends tell how he brought the knowledge of wine-making to humanity. His worshippers, who were mostly women, honoured him with frenzied rituals. Their behaviour often ran completely out of control. By drinking and dancing, they hoped to escape from the rules governing everyday life and to draw closer to the gods. Over the years, these rituals were included in religious festivals and helped to create Greek drama.

FAST TRACK
Zeus   p 8

These terracotta statues (below) show actors dressed for their roles on stage. Like all Greek actors, the man on the right is wearing a mask. This exaggerated his expression so that even people at the back of the theatre could see it.

FAMILY
Father Zeus
Mother Semele
Wife Ariadne

INSIDE STORY
Dionysus was once captured by pirates who demanded a ransom to set him free. However, far out at sea a miracle happened. Wine began streaming over the ship. The mast sprouted ivy-leaves, a bear appeared on deck and Dionysus turned into a lion. He sprang, roaring, at the pirate captain, who leaped overboard in terror with all the pirates. Dionysus then turned all of them into dolphins.

Terracotta statues of actors

THE THEATRE

The earliest Greek plays were performed in temples, in honour of the gods. They retold famous myths and legends, and also re-enacted important historical events. But these dramas became so popular that city-states built large open-air theatres, with room for all the thousands of spectators who wanted to watch. Many cities also awarded prizes for the best new plays. Only men could take part in Greek drama. City governments even banned women from attending certain performances. They believed that some plays were too rude, or too frightening, for women to watch.

Actors performed on a raised stage at the centre of a theatre (above). This was called an *orchestra*, which means 'dancing floor'.

Most Greek theatres were semi-circular (below). Tall rows of seats were arranged around a central space for the performers.

Greek actors (above) wore elaborate costumes, which might include wigs, padded clothes and 'tall' shoes with thick cork soles.

Admission to theatres was by ticket only. Usually, tickets took the form of bronze disks. Each was marked with a letter, to identify the block of seats where the ticket-holder was meant to sit. Wealthy Greek men often paid large sums of money to sponsor a theatre performance.

ASCLEPIUS
GOD OF HEALING: HEALTH AND MEDICINE

INSIDE STORY
Greek people told many different stories about Asclepius's early life. In one, he was abandoned by his mother on the slopes of a wild mountain, but was rescued and nourished by goats, guarded by a faithful dog. In another story, he was snatched from the flames of his mother's funeral pyre after she had been killed by the goddess Artemis. Then he was given to Cheiron, a wise and kindly Centaur. Cheiron cared for the young Asclepius, and taught him all he knew.

Asclepius was the god of healing. His father was Apollo but his mother was a human woman. Asclepius therefore lived on earth as a human and only became a god after his death. He was famous for his skill at healing the sick. Some of his powers were gifts from the gods – Athena gave him two flasks of blood, one of which could kill and the other bring the dead back to life. When Asclepius used this blood on his patients, Zeus became very angry and killed Asclepius with a thunder bolt.

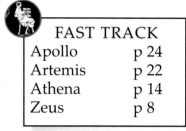

FAST TRACK
Apollo	p 24
Artemis	p 22
Athena	p 14
Zeus	p 8

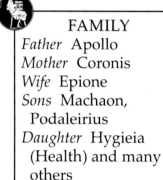

FAMILY
Father Apollo
Mother Coronis
Wife Epione
Sons Machaon, Podaleirius
Daughter Hygieia (Health) and many others

Asclepius was worshipped at many places, but his most important sanctuary was at Epidaurus in southern Greece (below). People travelled long distances to sleep in the temple there, hoping that Asclepius would appear to them in a dream and cure them. Asclepius's sacred symbol was the snake. Many snakes lived in his temple as honoured guests.

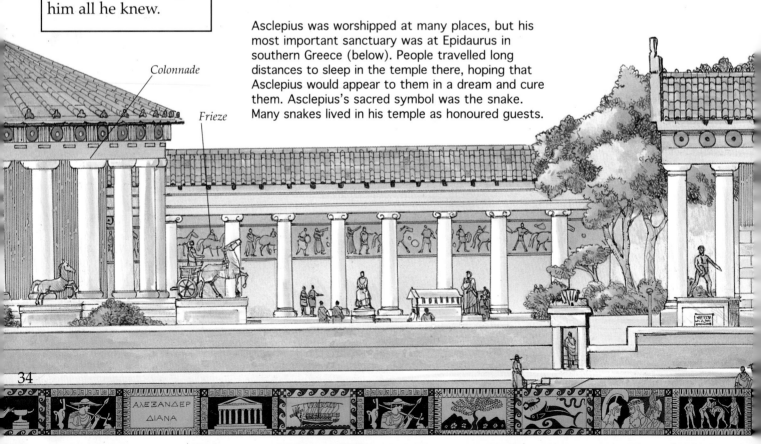

Colonnade

Frieze

GREEK MEDICINE

The Greeks believed that there were several different ways of trying to cure disease. They might ask the god Asclepius for help or they might visit a doctor. Greek doctors were very well trained. They studied how the body worked (although, by today's standards, they did not understand it very well). They were taught how to perform simple operations and how to make medicines from plants. They also learned how to observe their patients scientifically and were the first to recognise that a person's food, lifestyle, environment and even state of mind could all have an important effect on their health.

People who believed they had been cured by Asclepius gave thank-offerings to him (right). These were in the shape of the body-parts that had been healed and were hung on the wall of Asclepius's temple so that his spirit could see them. Thankful worshippers also left gifts of money in the temple's holy fountain and placed sacrifices of food on the temple altar.

One of Asclepius's daughters, Hygieia, was also worshipped after her death, as the goddess of good health. This carving (right) showing a leg that had been healed was made to hang in Asclepius's temple. Its inscription (carved writing) honours him, as well as Hygieia.

Temple

HADES
GOD OF THE UNDERWORLD: DEATH AND BURIAL

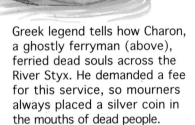

Greek legend tells how Charon, a ghostly ferryman (above), ferried dead souls across the River Styx. He demanded a fee for this service, so mourners always placed a silver coin in the mouths of dead people.

FAMILY
Father Cronus
Mother Rhea
Brothers Zeus, Poseidon
Sisters Demeter, Hera, Hestia
Wife Persephone

Hades was king of the Underworld – a cold and gloomy region inhabited by the souls of the dead. The Greeks described him as stern and grim but also merciful, just and fair. Hades had few dealings with people while they were alive. He did, however, lend his 'Cap of Darkness', which made the wearer invisible, to Athena and Hermes to help them in their adventures among humans. Very occasionally, he visited Earth, as when he carried away his bride, Persephone (see page 20).

A fierce three-headed dog called Cerberus (above) guarded the entrance to the Underworld. He posed no threat to newly-arrived dead souls – he only attacked souls who tried to leave.

When a family member died, women washed the body, sprinkled it with perfumed oils and herbs and then dressed it in clean white clothes, leaving the face uncovered. After a short time of mourning at home, it was carried on a cart (right) to a cemetery on the outskirts of a town. The funeral procession (which always took place before dawn) was accompanied by grieving relatives, dressed in black and with cropped hair. Women mourners sang funeral laments.

INSIDE STORY
Orpheus was the best musician in Greece. When his wife Eurydice died of a snake-bite, he went to the Underworld to bring her back to life. Hades liked his music so much that he agreed to set Eurydice free, as long as Orpheus did not look at her until they had left the Underworld. But Orpheus did look at Eurydice and she vanished. Orpheus was then doomed to a life of sorrow without her.

DEATH AND FUNERAL RITES

Life was short in ancient Greece. Most people could expect to live only until they were around 40 - that is just half as long as many Americans or Europeans today. Often, women died in childbirth, men died in battle or from accidental injuries and children died from infectious diseases. From time to time, deadly epidemics spread through whole communities, killing large numbers of people of all ages. When a Greek died, their body was either buried or cremated. The Greeks believed that a proper funeral was necessary to free a dead person's soul from their body. Family members therefore had an important duty to carry out funeral rites correctly, and with reverence and dignity.

This fine krater (below), made around 375 BC, is decorated with scenes showing mourners at a tomb. The young man who has died is shown standing in the arched doorway of his tomb, leaning rather sadly on his spear. Although the Greeks believed that it was glorious for young men to die bravely in battle, they also thought that life in this world was much better than any life after death could be.

Lions, symbols of strength and pride

Orpheus glances back at Eurydice (below) as they are leaving the Underworld.

Orpheus

Eurydice

Portrait of dead young man

Impressive doorway to tomb

Griffin

Griffins (above) were monster birds that were sacred to Zeus. They had the heads, wings and talons of eagles, and bodies like lions. Like other sky-monsters, they were constantly watchful and had exceptionally sharp eyesight. Legends told how they lived in lands to the north of Greece, where it was their duty to guard rich hoards of gold.

Greek myths are full of bold, handsome heroes, many of whom had superhuman powers. They had exciting adventures fighting monsters and human enemies. Greek writers and musicians wrote entertaining songs, poems and plays based on these myths, but they often had a deeper meaning as well. They made Greek people think about what it meant to be human, and about the strength and virtues they most admired in their gods.

The Sphinx (below) had the head and chest of a woman, the body and tail of a lion and the wings of a bird. It forced people to answer its riddles and killed those who got them wrong.

Sphinx

Medusa

Bellerophon

Pegasus

The Chimera (left) had the head of a lion plus a goat's head and body and a snake where its tail should be. It breathed fire at anyone who went near it, but it was killed by the hero Bellerophon, riding a magical horse that was called Pegasus.

The Gorgons were sisters called Stheno, Euryale and Medusa. They were the daughters of sea-monsters and had tusks like boars, gold wings, bronze hands and live snakes for hair. Their glance turned men to stone. Medusa (shown above) was killed by the hero Perseus. He used his shield as a mirror and cut off her head.

Chimera

MONSTERS

For the Greeks, monsters had a special meaning. They liked to contrast their own self-controlled behaviour with the mindless cruelty and brutality of monsters like the Sphinx, the Chimera and the Centaurs. It made them feel proud to be Greek. The story of fights between Greeks and Centaurs became particularly important after Greece was invaded by foreign troops (from Persia) in the 5th century BC. The Greeks regarded all foreigners as uncivilised barbarians. To celebrate their victory over the Persians, they created carvings of Centaurs being conquered by Greeks.

Centaurs were savage creatures; they were half-man and half-horse. It was rumoured that they fed on raw flesh, and were driven wild by the sight of women or the smell of wine. Like their close relatives the Satyrs, Centaurs had goats' beards, tails, hooves and shaggy legs.

INSIDE STORY
One myth described how the Centaurs fought the Lapiths – peaceful Greek people who lived in the mountains – and the Greek hero Heracles. Heracles killed the Centaurs with his poison-tipped arrows, but later they had their revenge. They tricked Heracles's wife into making him a poisoned shirt. Heracles put it on, and died in agony.

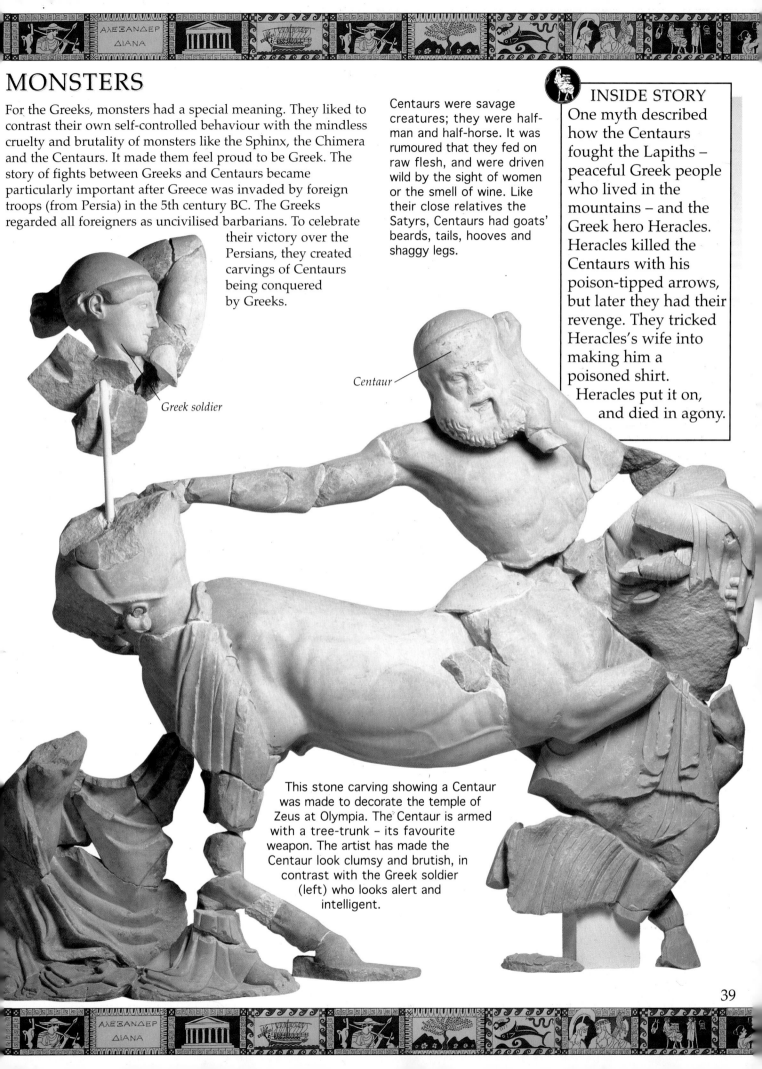

Greek soldier

Centaur

This stone carving showing a Centaur was made to decorate the temple of Zeus at Olympia. The Centaur is armed with a tree-trunk – its favourite weapon. The artist has made the Centaur look clumsy and brutish, in contrast with the Greek soldier (left) who looks alert and intelligent.

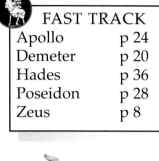

GODS

ALL AROUND

Family altar

The Greeks believed that they could bargain with the gods by offering them sacrifices (above). These included food and drink, incense, and valuable goods such as gold and silver and fine embroidered cloth. Many families offered small sacrifices at their own household altar every day. In return, they expected the gods to protect them from hunger, sickness and other misfortune.

Religion played a central part in Greek life and Greek citizens believed it was very important to keep in close contact with their gods. One of the ways that they did this was by holding festivals. Each city organised its own festivals to honour its favourite local gods. These took place at regular intervals during the year. Festival days were holy days – people stopped their normal work to chant hymns, take part in processions and share in sacred rituals.

The Greeks believed that Delphi, in central Greece, was the holiest place in the world. They visited a shrine there, dedicated to the god Apollo. They also consulted the Oracle (right) – a mysterious spirit that lived at Delphi, deep inside a cave. The Greeks believed it could foretell the future. The Oracle spoke through the mouth of the Pythia – a priestess who lived in Apollo's temple. After breathing in smoke from burning leaves, she answered questions handed to her by priests. They interpreted her answers to anxious listeners waiting nearby. According to Greek priests, Delphi was the *omphalos* (navel or centre) of the whole world. They placed a huge stone there to mark the centre point, and decorated it with strands of wool, to show that it was holy.

INSIDE STORY
The god Pan once chased a nymph called Syrinx. She ran away from him, until he trapped her by the side of a river. Syrinx called on the other gods for help, and they changed her into a clump of reeds. Pan felt very sad, until he heard the beautiful noise made by the wind blowing though the reeds. Pan then made a set of pipes from the reeds.

RITUALS

We do not know as much as we would like about Greek religion, because many rituals were held in secret. Sometimes – like festivals in honour of the corn-goddess Demeter – they were performed at night, deep underground. People taking part had to swear not to tell anyone about what happened during these celebrations, or to repeat the words of special secret prayers. If they did, the gods would curse them. They might also be punished by human laws. However, we do know how the Greeks prayed during public ceremonies. When speaking to the sky-gods, like Zeus and Apollo, they raised their hands up high. When praying to Hades, they turned their hands down, to face the ground. To ask blessings from the water-god Poseidon, they turned to face the sea.

The oldest Oracle in Greece was at Dodona, in the north-west. It was sacred to Zeus. The Greeks believed that if they wrote down a question (as above), Zeus would reply through the rustling of the leaves in a grove of oak-trees or through the cooing of doves perched in their branches.

For the Greeks, gods and goddesses were all around. They were usually invisible, but their power could be felt in mighty natural forces, such as the rumble of thunder, the sighing of the wind, or the crash of waves on the shore. They told stories (example left) about gods, nymphs and other supernatural spirits hidden in the world around them.

Few Greek people expected to meet their gods and goddesses face to face. That only happened to heroes in plays, or to people in poems, myths and legends. In spite of this, the Greeks had a very clear idea of what the gods and goddesses looked like. They were the same as ordinary men and women, but bigger and more beautiful – like the procession of gods and goddesses painted on this storage jar (left), made around 545-530 BC.

THE GAMES

FAST TRACK
Apollo	p 24
Hera	p 12
Zeus	p 8

Sport was an important part of education (above). Greek teachers aimed to produce 'a healthy mind in a healthy body'. Teachers might beat their students if they did not try really hard to win.

This bowl (below) is decorated with a scene from an Athenian sports festival around 400 BC. The goddess Nike (left) flies down to present the winner of a race with ribbons (Greek athletes tied these round their arms). The winner is carrying a lighted torch, which he has just used to light a holy fire on an altar at the end of the race track.

F or the Greeks, sports and religion were linked and sports contests formed part of many religious festivals. The most important sports festival was held at Olympia every four years. The first Olympic Games took place in 776 BC and by the 5th century BC, over 20,000 athletes, spectators and pilgrims travelled to Olympia from all over Greece. The games were organised by priests and judges kept a look-out for cheating. Marshals maintained law and order among the massive crowds of spectators.

Women were not allowed to attend the Olympic Games, although they could go to their own private female games, held every four years at Olympia in honour of Zeus's wife, Hera. A popular ancient Greek story told how one mother was so keen to see her son race that she disguised herself as a man and went to watch the Games in spite of the ban. However, she became so excited when she saw her son winning the race, that she shouted out, and was discovered.

INSIDE STORY
The goddess Nike's father was a Titan and her mother was the goddess of the River Styx. Nike spent most of her time helping Zeus, accompanied by her siblings, Striving, Strength and Power. Nike is usually portrayed as a young and beautiful woman, with graceful wings. She swooped down from the sky to save her favourites from danger or to reward victories in sport and in war.

Nike, goddess of victory

Winner

THE GAMES

Most games in honour of the gods lasted for five days. The first day was taken up with the opening ceremony and with religious rituals and sacrifices to the gods. Contests for young boys were also held then. The second day was devoted to horse and chariot racing, and to the pentathalon (running, jumping, throwing the discus and javelin, and wrestling). It ended with a parade of winners, followed by hymn-singing. On the third day, senior priests made important sacrifices and there was a public banquet. Foot-races were also held. The fourth day was the climax of sporting events, with wrestling and boxing competitions. On the fifth and final day, the winners received ribbons and wreaths. After the closing ceremony, everyone relaxed with a splendid feast.

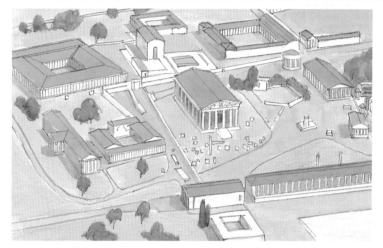

The vast sports complex at Olympia (above) contained Zeus's great temple, race tracks and a stadium where male spectators could watch the Games. There were also rooms for important visitors, a camp-site and space for market traders and food-sellers to pitch their stalls. Travellers to Olympia were protected by the 'Olympic Peace'. Priests taught that anyone who attacked them would be punished by Zeus.

Winners did not receive money prizes. They were given pottery, olive oil and fine cloth instead. But, because they brought honour to their towns and cities, they were sometimes rewarded with food and money when they returned home.

Most Greek athletes were amateurs. They took part in the games because they loved sport. However, there were a few professional sportsmen. They were paid by rich people, and spent months or even years training for just one event.

Like many other Greek sports, the *hoplitodromos* (race in armour, above) began as training for war. It was hot and very tiring. Greek athletes were naked for most other contests. It was cooler than being clothed and typical Greek loose robes would have hampered their movements.

GLOSSARY

Aulos Double flute.

Barbarian The Greeks' name for foreigners. They thought the languages spoken by non-Greeks sounded like 'bar-bar-bar'.

City-state Self-governing city or town and the surrounding countryside.

Colony Settlement in a foreign country.

Democracy City-state where the citizens ran the government.

Funeral pyre Large fire, on which dead bodies were ceremonially burned.

Funeral rites Prayers, songs, and offerings, designed to help a dead person's soul leave their body for the next world.

Golden Fleece Legendary sheep's fleece, full of gold.

Hoplite Foot-soldier.

Incense Substance burned to give off a sweet-smelling smoke.

Javelin Long spear.

Krater Large pottery bowl, used for mixing wine and water before drinking.

Lyre Musical instrument with strings, played rather like a harp.

Maenads Wild women, who worshipped Dionysus, the god of wine.

Muses Nine beautiful goddesses who encouraged the arts.

Nymph Nature spirit or minor nature-goddess.

Oracle A spirit that could see into the future.

Orchestra The central stage in a theatre, where the actors performed.

Parthenon A large temple in the centre of the Greek city-state of Athens, where the goddess Athena was worshipped.

Persians People from Persia (now Iran).

Traditional enemies of the ancient Greeks.

Phalanx A group of foot-soldiers, fighting side by side.

Pilgrim Someone who makes a journey for religious reasons.

Prophecy A forecast of future events.

Rituals Religious ceremonies, such as prayers, singing or chanting, and making offerings.

Sacrifices Offerings to the gods, to ask for help or blessings.

Sanctuary Holy place, often the innermost part of a temple.

Sceptre A special stick (or bar of metal or stone) carried by kings and queens as a sign of royal authority.

Shrine Holy place, where gods or goddesses are worshipped.

Terracotta Baked clay, used to make little statues and pottery.

Thesmophoria Religious festival, honouring the goddess Demeter, celebrated by women in Athens every year.

Thyrsus Long stick, or magic wand.

Trident A huge, deadly three-pronged fork.

Virgin Man or woman with no sexual experience.

Wet-nurse A woman who breast-feeds another woman's baby for pay.

INDEX